From: Funmi

USA Mothers' Day

Home Is Where Your Mom Is

Compiled by Evelyn Beilenson
Illustrated by Anne K. Higgins
Introduction by Suzanne Schwalb

PETER PAUPER PRESS, INC.
White Plains, New York

Illustrations copyright © 2009 Anne K. Higgins
www.artscounselinc.com

Designed by Heather Zschock

Copyright © 2009
Peter Pauper Press, Inc.
202 Mamaroneck Avenue
White Plains, NY 10601
All rights reserved
ISBN 978-1-59359-834-1
Printed in China
7 6 5 4 3 2 1

Visit us at www.peterpauper.com

Home Is Where Your Mom Is

Introduction

"Home" is a place inside
made of unconditional love,
comfort, and deep connection—
the things I feel when I'm with
you, Mom. You brought me
into this world, into a home
filled with love. You cared for
me, you guided me, you helped
me make my own way. All I've
achieved I've achieved because
of you. And no matter where
I go and what I do, I know

you're always "there" for me—
you're "home." As Oliver
Wendell Holmes once said,
"Where we love is home, home
that our feet may leave, but
not our hearts." Thank you,
Mom! I hope this little book
will let you know how much
you mean to me.

What is home without a mother?

ALICE HAWTHORNE

The moment a child is born
the mother is also born.
She never existed before.
The woman existed, but
the mother, never.
A mother is something
absolutely new.

RAJNEESH

Being a full-time
mother is one of the
highest salaried jobs . . .
since the payment
is pure love.

MILDRED B. VERMONT

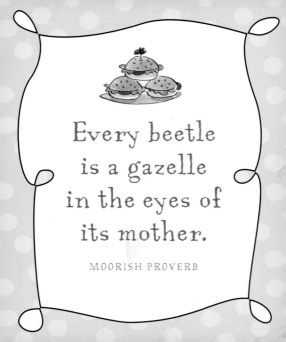

Every beetle
is a gazelle
in the eyes of
its mother.

MOORISH PROVERB

She never quite
leaves her children
at home, even when
she doesn't take
them along.

MARGARET CULKIN BANNING

Where we love
is home—
home that our
feet may leave,
but not our hearts.

OLIVER WENDELL HOLMES, SR.

Biology is the least of what makes someone a mother.

OPRAH WINFREY

You're not
famous until
my mother has
heard of you.

JAY LENO

There is no
way to be a perfect
mother, and a
million ways to
be a good one.

JILL CHURCHILL

You can choose
your friends,
but you only have
one mother.

MAX SHULMAN

Motherhood is
like Albania—
you can't trust the
descriptions in the books,
you have to go there.

MARNI JACKSON

A suburban
mother's role is to
deliver children
obstetrically once,
and by car
forever after.

PETER DE VRIES

The best way to keep
children at home is to
make the home
atmosphere pleasant,
and let the air out
of the tires.

DOROTHY PARKER

When it comes
to love,
Mom's the word.

A little girl,
asked where her
home was, replied,
"Where Mother is."

KEITH L. BROOKS

When I was a child,
my mother said to me,
"If you become a soldier,
you'll be a general.
If you become a monk
you'll end up as the pope."
Instead I became a painter
and wound up as Picasso.

PABLO PICASSO

I really
learned it all
from mothers.

DR. BENJAMIN SPOCK

The only thing a
lawyer won't question
is the legitimacy of
his mother.

W. C. FIELDS

The phrase "working mother" is redundant.

JANE SELLMAN

If you want your
children to turn
out well, spend twice
as much time with
them, and half as
much money.

ABIGAIL VAN BUREN

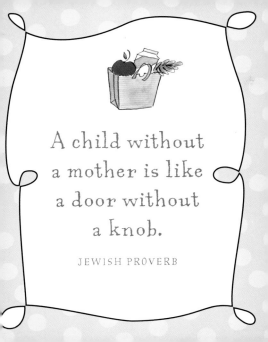

A child without
a mother is like
a door without
a knob.

JEWISH PROVERB

A mother is a person
who if she is not there when
you get home from school
you wouldn't know how
to get your dinner,
and you wouldn't feel
like eating it anyway.

AUTHOR UNKNOWN

My mother loved
children—
she would have
given anything
if I had
been one.

GROUCHO MARX

No matter how
old a mother is,
she watches
her middle-aged
children for signs
of improvement.

FLORIDA SCOTT-MAXWELL

All that I am,
or ever hope to be,
I owe to my
angel mother.

ABRAHAM LINCOLN

Any mother could
perform the jobs of
several air-traffic
controllers with ease.

LISA ALTHER

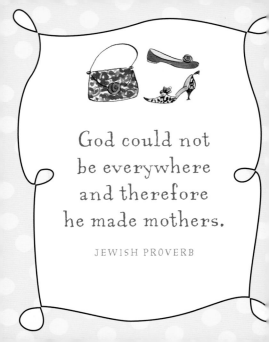

God could not
be everywhere
and therefore
he made mothers.

JEWISH PROVERB

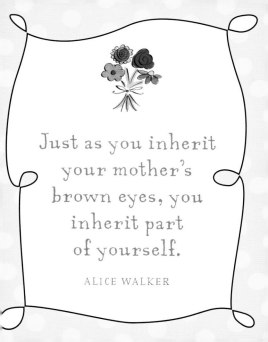

Just as you inherit
your mother's
brown eyes, you
inherit part
of yourself.

ALICE WALKER

Mother is the
name for God in the
lips and hearts of
little children.

WILLIAM MAKEPEACE THACKERAY

Some are kissing mothers
and some are scolding
mothers, but it is love just
the same, and most mothers
kiss and scold together.

PEARL S. BUCK

I think my life
began with waking
up and loving
my mother's face.

GEORGE ELIOT, Daniel Deronda

Mother—that was the bank where we deposited all our hurts and worries.

T. DE WITT TALMAGE

Cleaning your house while your kids are still growing is like shoveling the walk before it stops snowing.

PHYLLIS DILLER

The god to whom little boys say their prayers has a face very much like their mother's.

JAMES M. BARRIE

You become about as
exciting as your food
blender. The kids come in,
look you in the eye,
and ask if anybody's home.

ERMA BOMBECK

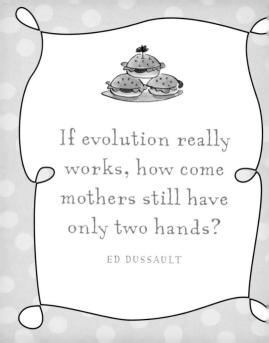

If evolution really works, how come mothers still have only two hands?

ED DUSSAULT

A mother starts out
as the most important
person in her child's
world and if she's
successful in her work,
she will eventually
become the stupidest.

MARY KAY BLAKELY

Mothers have to handle
all kinds of situations.
When presented with
the new baby brother he
said he wanted, the
toddler told his mother,
"I changed my mind."

JUDITH VIORST

You see much
more of your
children once they
leave home.

LUCILLE BALL

Motherhood is NOT for the faint-hearted. Used frogs, skinned knees, and the insults of teenage girls are not meant for the wimpy.

DANIELLE STEELE

At work, you think of the
children you have left at home.
At home, you think of the work
you've left unfinished. Such a
struggle is unleashed within
yourself. Your heart is rent.

GOLDA MEIR

The commonest fallacy
among women is that simply
having children makes one a
mother—which is as absurd as
believing that having a piano
makes one a musician.

SYDNEY J. HARRIS

The older I become,
the more I think
about my mother.

INGMAR BERGMAN

I never thought that
you should be
rewarded
for the greatest
privilege of life.

MAY ROPER COKER
1958 Mother of the Year

Motherhood
has a very
humanizing effect.
Everything gets
reduced to essentials.

MERYL STREEP

Motherhood has been the most joyous and important experience of my life. I would die for my children.

CARLY SIMON

The successful mother
sets her children free
and becomes more free
herself in the process.

ROBERT J. HAVIGHURST

A vacation frequently
means that the
family goes away for
a rest, accompanied
by mother, who sees
that the others get it.

MARCELENE COX

One good
mother is worth
a hundred
school masters.

GEORGE HERBERT

If you bungle raising
your children,
I don't think whatever
else you do well
matters very much.

JACQUELINE KENNEDY ONASSIS

"Working mother" is a misnomer. . . . It implies that any mother without a definite career is indolently not working, lolling around eating bon-bons, reading novels, and watching soap operas. But the word "mother" is already a synonym for some of the hardest, most demanding work ever shouldered by any human.

LIZ SMITH

My mother was a wit,
but never a sentimental one.
Once, when somebody in our
house stepped on our cat's paw,
she turned to the cat and said
sternly, "I TOLD you not
to go around barefoot!"

ZERO MOSTEL

Your children
are always your
"babies," even
if they have
gray hair.

JANET LEIGH

My mother was as
mild as any saint,
Half-canonized by
all that looked on her,
So gracious was her
tact and tenderness.

ALFRED, LORD TENNYSON

I figure that if the
children are alive
when I get home,
I've done my job.

ROSEANNE BARR

Men are what
their mothers
made them.

RALPH WALDO EMERSON

A mother is not
a person to lean on
but a person to make
leaning unnecessary.

DOROTHY CANFIELD FISHER

A man who has been the
indisputable favorite
of his mother keeps for life
the feeling of a conqueror,
that confidence of success
that often induces
real success.

SIGMUND FREUD

One of my children wrote
in a third-grade piece on how
her mother spent her time...
"one-half time on home,
one-half time on outside things,
one-half time writing."

CHARLOTTE MONTGOMERY,
Good Housekeeping, May 1959

In a child's
lunch basket,
a mother's
thoughts.

JAPANESE PROVERB

Beautiful as seemed
mamma's face, it became
incomparably more
lovely when she smiled,
and seemed to enliven
everything about her.

LEO TOLSTOY

Mama exhorted her children
at every opportunity to
"jump at de sun."
We might not land
on the sun, but at
least we would get
off the ground.

ZORA NEALE HURSTON

My mother was an
angel upon earth.
She was a minister of
blessing to all human
beings within her
sphere of action.

JOHN QUINCY ADAMS

Childish messages
on a mother's
refrigerator door could
fill a book of love.

LOIS KAUFMAN

Everybody's mother still cares.

LILLIAN HELLMAN